THE BEAUTIFUL WOMAN

WORKBOOK

Your Guide to Becoming

the Beautiful Woman You Already Are!

by Li Wang

Li Wang

liwangva@gmail.com

Published by EDMay, LLC, Waynesboro, VA

ISBN: 9781726709231

DEDICATION

This book is dedicated to Edd Schultz, my husband and primary supporter. He has helped me to become the confident, empowered, beautiful woman I am today.

CONTENTS

Author's Preface

I trembled as I stood before all those beautiful, powerful women. The Master of Ceremonies handed me the microphone. Taking a deep breath, I began speaking in my best "broken" English.

"Today, I'm here because I love the W.I.N. Foundation. W.I.N. Foundation help woman strong, confident. Eight year ago I come...I marry my American husband. I come here to America. I need be strong. I need go do something I can't do. So, English is not my native language. I go learning English. I have my company. I am Cosmo Model Ohio Agency CEO. Thank you, Dr. Tracy. Thank you."

I was Mrs. China Globe Classic 2015, competing against other women from all over the world in the Mrs. Globe Classic beauty pageant in Las Vegas, Nevada. The pageant is sponsored every year by the W.I.N. (Women In Need) Foundation, directed by Dr. Tracy Kemble. Her confidence in me had empowered me to have the confidence to be there.

My journey began in China. For more than twenty years, I was a primary school teacher of music and dance. In 2006, I met and married my American husband, Edd Schultz. We became acquainted on the **match.com** website. After a whirlwind online courtship, we were married within three months, in China. I had to wait 18 months before I was granted my visa to come to the United States.

A few years after we were married, Edd and I decided to pursue part time careers in modeling and acting. We enrolled in the Barbizon School of Modeling in Akron, Ohio. Several months later, I found myself working as a background actor (extra) in the movie *Captain America: The Winter Soldier*. I had my first experience as a runway model in a charity fashion show sponsored by Mothers Against Drunk Driving. More movies and fashion shows quickly followed. I set up a Facebook fan page and rapidly found myself with hundreds, then thousands of followers.

For the next several years, I was traveling not only to Cleveland and Columbus, but also to Pittsburgh, Indianapolis, New York City, Buffalo, Las Vegas, and even Hollywood to be in films, music videos, photoshoots, fashion shows, beauty contests, film festivals and even to judge beauty contests.

A pivotal moment for me was when I became Mrs. China Globe Classic 2015. Through Facebook, I became "friends" with Dr. Tracy Kemble, Founder and President of the Mrs. Globe and Mrs. Globe Classic beauty pageants. She asked me if I would like to represent my home country at the 2016 Mrs. Globe Classic competition in Las Vegas. I asked myself, "Why would she choose me?" Even though I was a model and actor, I felt that I was old and no longer attractive. But, Dr. Tracy encouraged me and my husband, Edd, gave me a push. It was because of their support and encouragement that I entered the competition and became Mrs. China Globe Classic 2015. For many months, leading up to the pageant, I made numerous personal appearances and gained more and more self-confidence. This kind of affirmation gave me the confidence I needed.

As Mrs. China Globe Classic, I met many wonderful people and had the opportunity to inspire other women. When I finally arrived at the pageant and met Dr. Tracy and my Globe Sisters, I felt immersed in a sea of love and support. Even though we were competitors, we were also sisters, encouraging, affirming, and supporting one another; celebrating each other as strong, confident, beautiful women.

I did not enter the pageant with the idea that I had to win. The most important part of the whole experience was feeling good about myself and being able to help others feel this way about themselves.

Later, I became the Talent Director for Cosmo Models Ohio, a local affiliate for Cosmopolitan Promotional Models, where I recruited, trained, and booked models and actors. It was a tremendous thrill for me to see people grow in their self-confidence. Now that I live in Virginia, I continue to act and model. This workbook is a way for me to reach out beyond my boundaries and touch the lives of women everywhere.

I decided to write this book because I discovered so many beautiful women in my journey, many of whom lacked assurance and confidence that they *were* beautiful. I felt that it was my mission to help empower these women and help them discover the beauty that is within them.

According to a recent global survey, only *four* percent of women consider themselves to be beautiful. But, even if we do not see our *own* beauty, interestingly enough, 80 percent of us believe that every woman has something beautiful about her.

When I was preparing to write this book, I reached out to my Facebook friends and asked them why they feel they are beautiful women. I explained that I was writing a book and wanted input from them. However, I only received a single response.

Many women do not see their own beauty because they lack self-confidence. Many women do not realize that they do not need to be "knock-out gorgeous" in order to be beautiful. As you will discover in the pages ahead, true beauty does not only involve outward appearance. True beauty begins inside a person and is then expressed outwardly.

Originally, I began to write this as a simple self-help book. The more I wrote, the more I realized that a workbook format would probably be more helpful than simple text. It is my hope that readers will take advantage of this format and use this book to stimulate action as well as thought.

I invite you to join me on this exciting journey of self-discovery.

- Li Wang

Foreword

When I sat down to read **The Beautiful Woman Workbook**, I didn't know what to expect. After all, Li Wang was sharing her wisdom and training in English, a foreign language to her. That, however, is what I feel is magical about this book. Li crosses international boarders and simply focuses on the elements of creating your own personal beauty regardless of ethnicity. This book is for any woman searching for both her outer image as well as her inner visibility. Job well done, Li. I am so proud of her path and the example of bravery that she is setting for women around the globe.

Dr. Tracy
President of Mrs. Globe

Chapter 1
What is Beauty?

The Merriam Webster dictionary defines beauty as "the qualities in a person or thing that give pleasure to the senses or mind."

We also frequently hear that "beauty is in the eye of the beholder."

This old maxim expresses the idea that beauty is subjective, rather than objective. Usually the first eye that beholds you every day is your own. Do you see yourself as being beautiful? If not, then self-image needs to be a top priority item for you.

Exercise: Write your definition of beauty.

There are many different criteria for beauty. Some of these criteria are based on iconic images. For example, balance and symmetry are often held in high regard when it comes to the human body. A small face with a large nose is not generally considered to be attractive. Large hands and large feet are not considered attractive. But then, that depends upon your cultural background.

Exercise: Make a list of physically beautiful criteria from an objective point of view.

Some criteria for beauty are based on cultural ideas and current trends. For example, in some cultures, height and weight are criteria for beauty. In other cultures, skin-tone, face shape, eye shape, and size are criteria for beauty.

Exercise: Search the internet for cultural criteria for beauty. List web sites below.

Exercise: Make a list of some cultural criteria for beauty.

When babies are born, people frequently say, "Oh, what a beautiful baby." To be honest, we must admit that many babies look like wrinkly little old people. They are not what we would normally term attractive little people. However, there is about them a quality of innocence, vulnerability, and simplicity that we do find attractive. It is their inner beauty that we perceive immediately. So, we can rightfully say, "Oh, what a beautiful baby."

Perhaps these criteria of innocence, vulnerability, and simplicity could also be applied to the beautiful woman.

Beauty is Only Skin Deep

You have probably heard this expression. But what does it mean? This maxim was first stated by Sir Thomas Overbury in his poem "A Wife" (1613): "All the carnall beauty of my wife is but skin-deep." I interpret this to mean that physical, outer beauty is not a measure of a woman's true beauty, which begins inside and manifests itself, in many ways, on the outside.

Also related to this is the idea of a "pretty woman". The word "pretty" is generally defined as being attractive in a delicate way. While pretty and beautiful are sometimes used interchangeably, one might say that a beautiful woman is not necessarily pretty and a pretty woman is not necessarily beautiful.

Exercise: What does "beauty is only skin deep" mean to you?

Attributes of a Beautiful Woman

There are many ways to describe a beautiful woman. A popular song once described a beautiful woman as "tall and tan and young and lovely." While this may be the song-writer's conception of a beautiful woman, it is not all-inclusive.

I would like to suggest a number of attributes (qualities that are considered an inherent part of, or necessary qualities of beauty) that may be appropriate. A beautiful woman is kind, confident, loving, and considerate. I will elaborate on these in a moment, but first....

Exercise: Make a list of what you believe are the two most important attributes of a truly beautiful woman. Then explain why you feel these attributes are appropriate.

Which of these attributes do *you* possess? Keep in mind, that attributes can be developed. Later, we will discuss making changes in your life. Perhaps some of the attributes that you listed above are ones to which you aspire.

Above, I mentioned what I consider to be four very important attributes for a beautiful woman: kind, attractive, confident, loving, and considerate. Now let's take a look at these for a moment.

A beautiful woman is *kind.* Kindness is consideration for others. Toleration, acceptance, courtesy, selflessness and understanding are indications of kindness. Selfish people are not often considered beautiful.

A beautiful woman is an *attractive* woman. What do we mean by *attractive*? Generally, this word is taken to mean "appealing to the senses." Surely, it is more than that. Magnets attract each other. They are drawn to each other. People are also drawn to (attracted to) one another. Why? For many reasons.

Of course, physical attractiveness is usually the first factor. We are initially attracted to people whom we find physically appealing. What makes up this appeal will, of course, vary from person to person. This goes back to our earlier idea that beauty is in the eye of the beholder.

We are also attracted to people who apparently give us what we need. If we are feeling powerless and someone makes us feel powerful – attraction. If we are feeling sad and someone makes us feel happy – attraction.

Familiarity is often a factor. We are attracted to what we already know or are used to or are comfortable with. This is often why people of a similar color, creed, ancestry, nationality, or age group are drawn to each other.

Common interests are also important. These allow us to participate in activities together, to spend more time with each other, and to feel comfortable with each other.

A beautiful woman is *confident.* We have previously addressed the issue of self-confidence.

Why is Beauty Important?

Exercise: List three reasons why it is important to *you* to be a beautiful woman.

1.

2.

3.

In order to be productive members of society, we need to be comfortable with ourselves. We need to feel that we are worthwhile. The more positive an attitude we have toward ourselves, the more worthwhile we feel. The more worthwhile we feel, the more worthwhile we become.

According to fashion photographer, Nigel Barker, "However outwardly attractive a woman may be, I promise you that what has attracted you to her is directly connected to whether she is confident, compassionate, honest, charming, energetic."

Exercise: Make a list of those whom you feel are the three most beautiful women.

1.

2.

3.

Exercise: Go online and find photos of your three most beautiful women.

Exercise: Why do you feel these women are beautiful?

1.

2.

3.

Exercise: What are the three most important things you have learned in this chapter?

1.

2.

3.

Exercise: What are three things that you will do as a result of what you have learned?

1.

2.

3.

Exercise: On a scale of 1 to 10, how do you feel about being a beautiful woman **now**?

1	2	3	4	5	6	7	8	9	10
Less Confident								More Confident	

CHAPTER 2

Four Levels of Personal Perception

Let us suppose that there are *Four Levels of Personal Perception*. We will be referring back to these throughout the workbook.

These four levels are:

The way we see ourselves (self-image)

The way others see us (other-image)

The way we think others see us (perceived-image)

The way we are (actual image)

For example, let's say Mary is 5'4". Mary may see herself as being short. Children might see her as being tall. Adults may see her as being short. Mary may think that others see her as being short, depending on the circumstances. In actuality, Mary is, indeed, average height according to American standards.

Self-image is one of the most powerful factors in determining who we are and how we will respond to those around us. Positive self image helps us to respond to the difficulties as well as the triumphs that we experience in life. It determines how we will react to stress as well as how we will form relationships with other people.

Our *other-image* has an effect on our self-image, in that this partially determines how other people will respond to us. Feedback is an essential element in forming our self-image.

Our *perceived-image* also affects our self-image because it, too, provides us with feedback, both positive and negative.

Then, there is the way things are. This "reality" may coincide with one of the three images above. Then again, it may not.

Of course, feedback can influence us both positively and negatively. For example, if a person is continually told that they are capable, confident, and attractive, chances are this is the way they will behave. On the other hand, if a person is continually told they are incapable, not confident, and unattractive, chances are *this* is the way they will behave.

Self-Image

Exercise: Write three things you feel about how you see yourself.

1.

2.

3.

Other-Image

Exercise: Write three things you feel about how you see yourself.

1.

2.

3.

Perceived-Image

Exercise: Talk to a trusted friend and ask that person to tell you three things about how others see you.

1.

2.

3.

Learned Helplessness

Learned helplessness is a condition in which a person suffers from a sense of powerlessness, arising from either a traumatic event or persistent feedback about failure to succeed. This theory was developed by psychologist Martin Seligman in the 1970s. It is thought to be one of the underlying causes of depression. For example, a well-meaning mother constantly tells her child that she is not doing a good job cleaning her room and, consequently, Mother cleans the room again. Soon the child learns that no matter what she does her mother will not be satisfied. This translates to "I may as well give up, because there is nothing that I can do to satisfy mother's criteria." This actually teaches the child that it is not necessary to clean her room, because Mother will do it anyway.

Exercise: List three ways in which you have learned to be helpless.

1.

2.

3.

Exercise: What are the three most important things you have learned in this chapter?

1.

2.

3.

Exercise: What are three things you will do as a result of what you have learned?

1.

2.

3.

Exercise: On a scale of 1 to 10, how do you feel about being a beautiful woman **now**?

1	2	3	4	5	6	7	8	9	10
Less Confident									More Confident

CHAPTER 3
Body

Human beings are a combination of body, mind, and spirit. In this book, we will explore the concept of beauty in these three modes. These modes are integrally related to one another.

Let us start with outward appearance. Of course, your body is what everyone sees. It is through your body that you express what is in your mind and heart. So, it stands to reason that your body is the prime means of expressing your beauty. We shall approach the body in two ways: nature (inherited) and nurture (learned).

Nature

You were born with a certain kind of body. You inherited this from your parents. You are tall, short, or in between. You have brown, blue, green or hazel eyes. You have brown, black, red or blond hair. You have a certain body shape, such as straight, hourglass, pear, etc. You are thin, plump or average. Sometimes this depends upon your frame (your skeletal structure). There are various features on your face (long nose, upturned nose, small or large ears, full or thin lips) that are inherited.

EXERCISE: List several of your *inherited* body characteristics.

1.

2.

3.

Studies have shown that there are three major body types: Ectomorph, Endomorph, Mesomorph. The *Ectomorph* is usually very slim with a light build and small joints. Shoulders also tend to be thin. The *Endomorph* is usually solid with short arms and legs, and tend to be referred to as "stocky." The *Mesomorph* is usually strong, athletic and muscular.

Most people do not fit definitively in one of the three types, but are usually a combination of at least two. Body type can also affect how you gain or lose weight, because of the metabolism associated with each.

EXERCISE: Search the internet for information about body types. Write the URL(s) below. Which one describes you?

Nurture

Even though you are born with certain physical traits, many of these can be changed through diet, exercise, surgery, injections, or other means. You can make decisions about what you would like to change.

EXERCISE: List any body characteristics that you *have* changed.

EXERCISE: List any body characteristics that you *would like to* change.

Later, we will give you tools to help you make these changes.

Nutrition

It may be cliché to say, "you are what eat," but there is, of course, a certain amount of accuracy in this statement. While we do not have to become fanatical about our diet, it is important to be informed and to be responsible.

Healthy Eating = Healthy Living

Let us begin this section with a short inventory. Using the following chart, record a sample of what you normally eat.

Exercise: Meal Inventory

Typical Breakfast	Typical Lunch	Typical Dinner

Exercise: List what type of snacks you usually eat.

When You Eat

When you eat is just as important as *what* you eat. Your body is like a machine, but it is more complex than a simple engine or motor. This machine needs a steady source of energy throughout the day. You don't just fill up the tank in the morning and off you go. Of course, most Americans are used to not filling the tank in the morning. We eat a small breakfast, if any, then eat a big lunch and a bigger dinner. Unfortunately, this is not necessarily beneficial for the "body machine."

Exercise: Using the chart below, indicate *when* you normally eat.

Breakfast	Lunch	Dinner

Exercise: List when you usually eat snacks (and what you usually snack on).

Snacks	Snacks	Snacks

The body needs a steady source of fuel throughout the day. So, eating every three hours is what is recommended. This way the metabolism keeps steady and burns calories as the day goes on. The body also knows that it is being given sufficient fuel, so it does not have to go into "survival mode" and hang on to fat. That's right. When the body does not receive enough fuel (food) it becomes confused and hangs onto fat because it does not know when it will be fed again. Starvation diets are usually counterproductive.

Eating every three hours might seem like a lot, but we are not talking about actual meals. Three meals and three snacks will help to maintain a healthy metabolism, especially when protein is a part of each meal or snack. For example:

1. Breakfast – bowl of oatmeal with crushed nuts and milk

2. Snack – cheese or nuts

3. Lunch – tuna salad (onion, tomato, lettuce) sandwich on whole wheat bread, carrot or celery sticks

4. Snack – hard-boiled egg

5. Dinner – baked chicken, potato, and vegetable

6. Snack – whole wheat bread with a sprinkle of olive oil

Filtered water, tea or freshly squeezed fruit juice are suggested beverages. Be responsible when using other beverages such as coffee, soda, wine, etc. Watch the sugar, caffeine, and alcohol content carefully. Any of these in excess can be detrimental. Avoid "diet" drinks. They were created as an alternative to sugary drinks with lots of calories. However, studies have shown that many artificial sweeteners can have adverse effects on your health. Also, when you drink an artificially sweetened beverage, your brain says, "Yeah! I just got some sugar." But, then it realizes that this was not true sugar, causing the body to crave the real thing. High fructose corn syrup has also been shown to cause cravings for MORE!

The last snack of the day need not include protein, because your body is winding down and is about to rest.

When you eat throughout the day, you end up not feeling hungry. This, in turn, helps you to not overeat.

Supplement this schedule of eating with eight servings of water (8 oz. each) throughout the day.

How Much You Eat

How much you eat at each meal is equally as important as what and when. The American formula for eating usually is:

1. Breakfast – small, if any

2. Lunch – big

3. Dinner – bigger

When you think about it, this does not make a lot of sense. When you wake up in the morning, your body needs fuel, energy. So, a big breakfast would be in order. In the middle of the day, for lunch, you still need a good amount of fuel to get you through the rest of the day. But, not so much that your body has to work overtime on digestion (making you sluggish and sleepy). At dinner, your body is preparing to rest, so it does not need very much fuel. In fact, if it gets too much food, it will need to spend a lot of time and energy digesting that food during sleep, when your body needs to rejuvenate itself.

There is an old saying about how to eat:

⊀ Breakfast like a king

⊀ Lunch like a prince

⊀ Dinner like a pauper

Imagine your eating pattern as being like a pyramid. If you eat a lot in the morning, less for lunch, and less for dinner, you have a triangle. Put a reverse triangle on top of that and you get an hour-glass figure. That's the kind of "figure" that you will have. If, however, you use the typical American formula, you will have an upside-down triangle. Reverse that and put it on top and look at the diamond-shaped figure. That's the kind of "figure" that you will have. The choice is yours. Hour glass or diamond?

Exercise: Describe your normal size meals

Breakfast	Lunch	Dinner

Exercise: Put on a bathing suit and stand in front of a full-length mirror. Scan yourself from head to toe. How do you feel about what you see?

Remember that what you see is partially a product of genetics and partially a product of your own personal stewardship.

That stewardship not only includes what you eat, but also what you do. The human body is meant to be exercised in order to keep it fit. The mere act of walking and moving are forms of exercise.

Also, keep in mind that an attractive figure is not just about physical beauty. It is also an indication of physical health. Before trying to make any changes in your physical body be sure to consult your physician. Some physical characteristics may be indications of underlying health problems. Check for such things as thyroid problems, diabetes, etc. Such ailments often have a profound effect on our physical appearance.

Exercise

Another essential element of keeping your body healthy is exercise. While I do not advocate becoming an exercise fanatic, we all need physical activity to keep the physical machine running well. Exercise gives us energy. It also helps us maintain our muscles and organs. There are many ways that we can exercise, including yoga, Pilates, Zumba, calisthenics, sports, and just plain walking. Many ailments such as heart disease and stroke can be prevented with sufficient exercise. Keeping your heart strong and your circulation powerful will help to allow your body to perform at its best.

Exercise: List what kinds of exercise you do on a regular basis.

Remember that before you embark on any new kind of exercise regime, you should check with your doctor. Too much exercise, or the wrong kind of exercise, can often do more harm than good.

The Centers for Disease Control and Prevention recommend three possible formulas for **weekly** exercise.

Two hours and thirty minutes of moderate intensity aerobic activity (such as brisk walking).

*Muscle strengthening activities (such as resistance training) on **two or more days a week** that work all major muscle groups.*

-or-

One hour and fifteen minutes of vigorous-intensity aerobic exercise (such as jogging or running).

Muscle strengthening activities (such as resistance training) on two or more days a week that work all major muscle groups.

-or-

An equivalent mix of moderate and vigorous aerobic activity.

Muscle strengthening activities (such as resistance training) on two or more days a week that work all major muscle groups.

You Are What You Consume

Earlier we said that "you are what you eat." Perhaps it would be more accurate to say that "you are what you consume." Our personality and our appearance are determined by what we take into ourselves on a number of different levels. As we mentioned above, the food that you eat helps to shape your physical body. We also consume using all of our physical senses: sight, hearing, taste, touch, smell.

Sight - Everything that we see makes some kind of impression on us. When you look at yourself in a mirror, you see yourself as you really are. This sight can inspire feelings of self-confidence, pride, frustration, anger, etc. These feelings result in either our taking action to change what we see, or our ignoring what we see.

We also watch television and movies, as well as read, and perhaps even play a few video games (don't tell your kids!). When we do this, we are consuming and we are influencing who we are. Think about the content of these activities. Do you read for enjoyment? Education? Both? What kind of movies do you watch? Romance? Fantasy? Sci-Fi? Documentaries? What kind of TV programs do you watch? News? Comedies? Game Shows? Reality TV? Cooking shows? Shopping channels? Sports?

Exercise: Make a list of books you have recently read. How do they make you feel?

Exercise: Make a list of movies you have recently watched. Why do you like them? How do they make you feel?

Exercise: Make a list of TV programs you have recently watched. Why do you like them? How do they make you feel?

Exercise: Carefully consider your reading and watching habits. Reflect below on why you read and watch what you do and how you feel about this. Do you read and watch for enjoyment? Education? Inspiration? Recreation? Do you watch or read too little or too much?

Hearing - everything we hear makes some kind of impression on us. When we hear joyful music, we may feel inspired. We may have more energy. We may have more motivation. When we hear sad music, we may feel depressed. When we hear an uplifting conversation, we may be inspired. When we hear a comedian telling jokes, we may feel happy. When we hear arguments or abusive remarks, we may feel angry or depressed.

Exercise: What is your favorite kind of music and why?

Exercise: Make a list of your three favorite songs. Why do you like them? How do you feel when you listen to them?

Taste - Back to food again! We tend to eat foods that we enjoy. Flavor is important to our enjoyment. There are also some foods that we may not feel taste good, but we know they are beneficial.

Exercise: What are your three favorite foods? Why do you enjoy them?

Touch – We all have different feelings about touching and being touched. Some of us are huggers, while others prefer not to participate in this kind of display of affection, for various reasons. Kissing and caressing customs may vary within cultures and even families. Everyone needs a certain amount of personal space. Some people prefer a lot, while others accept less. We need to understand and respect this.

Exercise: How much personal space do you need? How comfortable are you with public displays of affection?

Smell – Do you wear perfume or cologne? Why? During some periods of history, people wore scents to mask body odor. Later, people used scent to attract the opposite sex, or simply to feel good about themselves.

Of the five senses, the sense of smell is the most powerful. Think for a moment about the smell of fresh roses or of fresh-baked bread. Then, think about the smell of garbage. You will react in two very different ways. Imagine the person standing to your right smelling of clean, fresh linen and the person to your left smelling of rotten eggs. To whom would you turn for advice?

Exercise: Reflect below on how smell affects your life.

Exercise: What are the three most important things you have learned in this chapter?

1.

2.

3.

Exercise: What are three things that you will do as a result of what you have learned?

1.

2.

3.

Exercise: On a scale of 1 to 10, how do you feel about being a beautiful woman **now**?

1	2	3	4	5	6	7	8	9	10
Less Confident									More Confident

CHAPTER 4
Mind

In the late 1950s, psychologist Eric Berne developed a personality theory that he called Transactional Analysis. One of the major ideas in this theory is that there are four "life positions" that we can potentially adopt throughout our lives.

I'm OK - You're OK: I accept myself as being worthwhile; and I accept others as being worthwhile.

I'm OK - You're not OK: I accept myself as being worthwhile; I do not accept others as being worthwhile.

I'm not OK - You're OK: I do not accept myself as being worthwhile; I accept others as being worthwhile.

I'm not OK - You're not OK: I do not accept myself as being worthwhile; I do not accept others as being worthwhile.

The first position is the one we should all strive for. It is the healthiest position.

The second position fosters an attitude of "I am better than you." This is not a healthy position, because it leads to feelings of superiority. It does not affirm the value of other persons.

The third position fosters an attitude of "Everyone is better than I."

This is not a healthy position, because it leads to feelings of inferiority and eventually to depression. It does not affirm the value of your self as a person. Interestingly enough, this is the position into which we are born. As infants, we are totally dependent (I'm not OK) upon our caregivers (You're OK). Hopefully, our caregivers do their job well, and they foster within us a sense of "I'm OK" rather than "I will *always* be dependent upon others (aka I'm not OK)." If they are abusive or neglectful, this could eventually lead to a sense of I'm not OK – You're not OK."

The fourth position fosters an attitude of hopelessness. This is obviously not a healthy position. It ultimately leads to despair; perhaps even suicide.

As a beautiful woman, you should aspire to the first position, I'm OK-you're OK. A truly beautiful woman sees the beauty in herself as well as in others.

Exercise: Which position do you feel you are in now? Why?

Self-Image

The French philosopher René Descartes once said, "I think, therefore, I am." Of course, he was trying to prove his own existence. Consider where he started. He started with his mind, with a mental construct. "If I am capable of thought, I must exist." The logical extension of this premise that "I think, therefore, I am" is, "I think. Therefore, I am a thinking thing."

Another logical extension is that "I think, therefore, I am what I think I am."

Our self-perception helps to create our reality. Joanne thinks that she is very confident; therefore, she behaves in a confident manner, which in turn causes her to become a confident person.

Exercise: What do you think *you* are?

Examples: I think I am a lazy person.

Therefore, I am a lazy person.

I think I am an honest person.

Therefore, I am an honest person.

I think I am:

Therefore, I am:

I think I am:

I think I am:

Therefore, I am:

Conscious versus Subconscious Mind

The human mind has two major aspects, the conscious mind and the subconscious mind. The conscious mind is the part of us that is immediately aware of our existence and our environment. When we are awake, we are primarily using our conscious mind.

Our subconscious mind lies below the surface. This part of our mind deals with emotions, memories, and parts of our being of which we are not immediately aware. When we are asleep we are primarily using our subconscious mind.

The subconscious includes a repository of all our thoughts, feelings, and emotional experiences. Think of it as the hard drive for the computer that is our brain/mind. The conscious mind is like the person who sits down at the key-board.

For better or worse, the human brain/computer has built-in voice recognition. This means data enters the hard drive not only through the key-board (conscious mind), but also through the rest of the outside world by means of our five physical senses: sight, hearing, taste, touch, and smell.

When we are young, our brain is like a tape recorder that is permanently in record mode. It is not sophisticated enough to filter any input. All of the experience that it records by means of the five physical senses will be stored in the subconscious mind.

At some point in our development, we begin to develop a sort of filter between the conscious and subconscious minds. Let us call this filter the critical mind. When information comes in through the conscious mind, it is instantly analyzed by the critical mind, which will then either accept or reject this information.

Part of the process of analyzing this information is an instantaneous search of the data stored in the subconscious mind. For example, you encounter a dog. The critical mind conducts a search of all the data related to "dog" that is found in the subconscious mind.

Let us say that when you were young you had a family dog. This dog was loving, affectionate, and well-trained. There will be a great deal of positive emotion surrounding this experience of "dog." So, you will probably respond positively to the dog.

Exercise: List three positive memories of which you are aware.

1.

2.

3.

On the other hand, your primary experience of "dog" may have been your neighbor's big German Shepherd pouncing on you, knocking you over and biting your face. With this kind of emotionally charged negative experience in your subconscious mind, you will probably respond to this dog with fear. Even if the conscious mind says, "It is only a dog," the programming in the subconscious mind is so emotionally charged that it is more powerful. This is how many phobias are created.

Exercise: List three negative memories of which you are aware.

1.

2.

3.

Subconscious influence is often more powerful because it is more spontaneous, and we do not have as much conscious control.

Within the subconscious mind, there is also a primitive safeguard known as the fight, flight, or freeze response. When we sense any kind of danger, this response happens automatically, without conscious control.

You are confronted by a fierce dog. Your subconscious mind goes into fight, flight or freeze mode. You react with one of the three responses. Fight: you attack the dog. Flight:

you run away from the dog. Freeze: you stand still, hoping the dog will go away or not notice you. Which one of these responses actually happens, depends upon your subconscious programming. You do not simply stand there and rationally think, "Let's see. What are my options?" You automatically respond. Automatically means without conscious decision making.

Our cave-dwelling ancestors relied upon this response for their survival. Now we are more sophisticated. But, often we let this survival response just take over. How do we change that? By preparing ourselves subconsciously.

Exercise: List three ways in which you have experienced the fight, flight, or freeze response.

1.

2.

3.

Both aspects of our consciousness have a profound effect on who we are.

Confidence

Confidence is an awareness of one's own power; an awareness of one's ability to do, say, and think whatever is most appropriate in any situation. If you are confident, you will be able to do whatever you need to do in any situation.

In 1936, Dale Carnegie wrote an influential book entitled **How to Win Friends and Influence People**. In his introduction, he explained why he wrote the book. For many years, he had been teaching people the art of public speaking. "But gradually, as the seasons passed, I realized that as sorely as these adults needed training in effective speaking, they needed still more training in the fine art of getting along with people in everyday business and social contacts."

Many people have a fear of public speaking, for several possible reasons. They may feel they are not prepared to say the right thing. They may feel they are not qualified to say the right thing. They may feel that people will not respect them as being qualified to speak on the subject. They may feel they lack sufficient polish and poise to speak in front of a group. In short, they may not be aware of their own abilities. They may well lack self- confidence.

Exercise: On a scale of 1 to 10, estimate your level of overall self-confidence									
1	2	3	4	5	6	7	8	9	10
Not very self-confident								Very self-confident	

Building self-confidence is not necessarily an easy task. This actually begins in our childhood, when we are being molded and formed by those around us. Our parents (and siblings, if we have any) are our first teachers. When we perform any actions, the feedback that we receive from our parents determines how we will act again. For example, a baby reaches out to touch a hot stove. This is a simple act of curiosity. If the baby touches the hot stove, which causes pain, the baby will learn not to touch a hot stove again. If the mother screams, "No, no, no!" the child may possibly learn a number of things. First, baby may learn not to be curious. Second, baby may learn not to reach out without Mother's permission. There are many things that baby may learn depending upon the feedback that he/she receives from Mother.

If a child is constantly criticized, then he/she may have difficulty becoming aware of his/her ability to behave correctly in any situation. On the other hand, if a child is rewarded for positive, acceptable behavior, then the child is likely to repeat that kind of behavior. All of this impacts self-confidence.

Exercise: List three ways in which you were criticized when you were young.

1.

2.

3.

Exercise: List three ways in which you received positive feedback when you were young.

1.

2.

3.

Changing Actions/Changing Feelings

Feelings follow actions. You prepare a delicious meal. You feel good. You back your car into a tree. You feel bad. One of the ways to boost your self-esteem is to do things that will make you feel good about yourself. What interests you? What are your hobbies? What are your skills? You can build your self-confidence by building on your successes.

Start with small achievements. Do something simple that you know you can do well. Sit back for a moment and enjoy your success. Continue this until you have been able to achieve at least three small successes. Then go on to something bigger and more complicated. Each time you achieve a success, give yourself a reward. This reward can be something very simple.

Being rewarded for a success will lead to other successes. More details on this process later.

Exercise: List three actions that you can take to change negative feelings about yourself.

1.

2.

3.

Exercise: What are the three most important things you have learned in this chapter?

1.
2.
3.

Exercise: What are three things that you will do as a result of what you have learned?

1.
2.
3.

Exercise: On a scale of 1 to 10, how do you feel about being a beautiful woman now?

1 2 3 4 5 6 7 8 9 10
Less Confident   More Confident

CHAPTER 5
Spirit

"Spirituality" is defined by The Merriam Webster dictionary as "sensitivity or attachment to religious values." The term "religious values" implies some kind of relationship to "the divine", however you think of that. This becomes a complex issue since there are many concepts of "the divine". Some of these include a personal divinity, while others include a more non-personal "cosmic consciousness" idea. Whatever your belief is, it may (or may not) affect how you live your life.

This workbook is not meant to be a deep, theological treatise, but rather a means to help you achieve the goal of realizing and actualizing your inner beauty. So, we will simplify our definition of spirituality to be "how you relate to the world beyond yourself."

Let's begin with a "spiritual" inventory.

Exercise: Spiritual Inventory

1. Do you believe in a personal Greater Power? If so, why? Describe it.

2. Do you believe in some form of prayer and/or meditation? If so, what?

3. Do you believe in some form of divine plan? Destiny? Fate? If so, why?

4. Do you believe that all people are part of a spiritual family with the Divine as the Parent? If so, why?

5. Do you belong to any kind of organized religious community ? If so, what and why?

6. If you answered "yes" to 5, do you attend religious services?

7. If you answered "yes" to 5, does your religious life require you to do any kind of outreach or fellowship?

8. Do you read any kind of spiritual literature? If so, what, and what do you feel that you gain from it?

9. Do your religious beliefs teach you to behave in a certain way toward other people? If so, what?

Your answers to these questions can help you to determine what kind of spiritual life you have or do not have. Why is this important and what does it have to do with being a beautiful woman? Your spirituality does not only have to do with how you relate to the divine, it also has a great deal to do with how you relate to other people.

For example, if you are affiliated with a religious group, this group probably has strong feelings about how other people should be treated. "Love your neighbor in the same way that you love yourself." This commandment implies first that you love yourself. Self-love is not selfish. Remember our previous reference to "I'm OK – You're OK"? It is healthy to have positive self-regard and self-respect. Other people are naturally attracted to a person who has self-respect. Self-confidence is usually a byproduct of self-respect.

Most religious groups foster a sense of community. They care for one another, so support one another when they are in need or in trouble. Healthy religious groups do not foster a sense of "us against them". That is an "I'm OK – You're not OK" position, and that is not healthy.

Exercise: What are the three most important things you have learned in this chapter?

1.

2.

3.

Exercise: What are three things that you will do as a result of what you have learned?

1.

2.

3.

Exercise: On a scale of 1 to 10, how do you feel about being a beautiful woman **now**?

1	2	3	4	5	6	7	8	9	10

Less Confident   More Confident

CHAPTER 6

Beauty is as Beauty Does

True beauty is measured not only by your appearance, but also by your actions.

There is a popular saying that has been with us since the 14th century: "Beauty is as beauty does." This can be found in many forms and many works of literature, including Chaucer's **Canterbury Tales**. The idea is that being a truly beautiful person is not just about physical appearance, it is also about personality.

A woman can be physically unattractive, but have a magnanimous personality. On the other hand, a woman can be physically attractive, but have a terrible personality. As mentioned before, the kind of person you are is profoundly affected by the way you are treated by other people from your birth on. Frequently, people with unattractive personalities are those who have been mistreated, abused or neglected in some way. These are people who are stuck in the I'm not OK – You're OK or the I'm not OK – You're not OK life positions.

One of the goals of this workbook is to help you reinforce your feelings of I'm OK – You're OK.

So, what does "beauty do?" Let's begin with *your* thoughts on the subject.

Exercise: Write three things that you believe a beautiful woman should do.

1.

2.

3.

In the 1950s, Walt Disney Studios produced a popular children's TV series called *The Mickey Mouse Club*. In one episode, Mouseketeer Doreen Gillespie sang a short song entitled *Beauty is as Beauty Does* as part of a segment on "words to grow by." The lyrics simply stated that if you want to be beautiful, then you should be kind to other people.

During my reign as Mrs. China Globe Classic 2015, one of the expectations was that I would make personal appearances to promote the pageant and the sponsoring W.I.N. Foundation, as well as to empower women. This was one of the most enjoyable aspects of my reign. At Christmas time, I visited an assisted-living facility and made it a point to visit those women residents who did not usually have visitors or family, and I gave them each a small gift. The response was overwhelming. There were many tears and a lot of appreciation. This helped *me* to feel empowered. The gift of giving love and attention to the lonely made me feel more like a beautiful woman. Volunteer and charitable working/giving are reciprocal occasions.

Exercise: Think of a few ways that *you* can share yourself with others.

1.

2.

3.

Deportment and Fashion

An attractive young woman walks down the street. She's chewing gum. Her shoulders are slouched. Her head is slightly bowed. Eyes are looking down at the ground. What does all this say to the onlooker? Does she seem confident? Does she seem happy? Does she seem energetic? Probably not.

An average-looking young woman walks down the same street. Her shoulders are back. Her head is up; she looks forward and occasionally makes eye contact with other people who are walking by. What does all this say to the onlooker? She appears to be a self- confident person and will probably be noticed more readily than the first woman.

Deportment is about how you conduct yourself; how you walk, how you talk, how you dress; your behavior in various situations. This also includes your attitude.

The famous choreographer George Balanchine is said to have told many of his ballet students, "Proud is allowed, but haughty is naughty." In other words, it is perfectly appropriate for a person to be proud of their accomplishments, but they should not be arrogant. Pride is a component of self-confidence. "Pride" is a feeling of satisfaction derived from one's own achievements. This is simply acknowledging reality for what it is.

Some people feel that humility can be expressed by self-denial. You have just finished a painting. You hang it on the wall.

Friend: *That's beautiful. You did a wonderful job.*

You: *Oh, no. I could have done much better. It's not my best work.*

Friend: *Oh, but it really is beautiful.*

You: *No, no, no. In fact, I think it's terrible.*

Friend: *It's not terrible. I really like it.*

You: *No, I think I'll take it down.*

Friend: *Please don't.*

It may appear on the surface that you are being humble. However, upon closer inspection, it becomes apparent that you are fishing for compliments.

You: *I think that's the most wonderful painting I've ever done.*

Friend: *Yes, it is very nice.*

You: *It shouldn't be on my wall, it should be in a museum.*

Friend: *(speechless)*

You: *It is marvelous. In fact, it's better than anything that anyone else could do.*

Friend: *(speechless)*

This is certainly a situation in which you are being arrogant, haughty...naughty.

Friend: *That's a beautiful picture. You did a wonderful job.*

You: *Thank you.*

This is the most appropriate response. You are acknowledging that you did a good job. You are also acknowledging that your friend appreciates your endeavors. You are showing confidence in your own ability, without being consumed by pride. This is true humility.

Deportment also has to do with such things as etiquette and table manners. While to some this may seem overly fussy, please remember that *other-image* does affect *self-image*. I once observed a well-dressed woman eating breakfast in a restaurant. She was cutting pancakes. She held the fork in her left hand as though it were a pitchfork. Whenever she chewed, her mouth was wide open. Uncomfortable, to say the least. What may seem like harmless habits to us might have an impact on how others see us. Smoking, chewing gum, using foul language. Ask yourself if these activities make you feel and look like a confident, beautiful woman.

Exercise: Do an online search for websites that describe table manners and etiquette. How do you measure up? What can you do to improve your deportment?

To paraphrase another cliché, "Clothes don't make the man or woman." While clothes do not *make* you who you are, they do *reflect* who you are, or at least, who you feel you are (self-image). When we are children, our parents decide what we will wear. After a certain age in our development, we are able to choose our own wardrobe. It is at that point in our lives we have an opportunity to show the world who or what we think we are. We may decide to always wear casual clothes, so that we can reflect a relaxed attitude towards life or we may decide to dress in a formal way to reflect a professional-businesslike attitude.

We also are free to choose different wardrobes according to the circumstances in which we find ourselves. If you are spending the afternoon food shopping, you may choose to wear jeans and a sweatshirt. However, if you are going to a job interview for a position as an accounting clerk, you may choose to wear a business suit.

Exercise: What kind of clothes do you like to wear at home?

Exercise: What kind of clothes do you like to wear for social occasions?

Choosing the right clothes for yourself (fashion) is a bit of an art and a bit of a science. Certain colors or hues can have an effect on how you look. For example, Dark colors tend to give the appearance of being slimmer. White and light colors tend to give the appearance of being heavier. This is purely an optical illusion, but it does affect your other-image.

Similarly, certain colors may compliment or not compliment different skin tones. Skin tones may be light or dark, or variations in between. If you have light-toned skin and you wear a bright yellow blouse, your face may appear jaundiced, for example. If your skin is a dark tone and you wear black, you may appear to be darker than you really are.

Exercise: Do an online search to find what your skin tone is considered.

My skin tone is:

Exercise: After doing online research, write below what colors are best suited for your skin tone.

The color of your clothing is important; so is the style. When I say "style" at this point, I am not talking about trends, but what basic styles will compliment your coloring, body type and age. For example, if you are a forty-year-old woman who is slightly overweight, I would not recommend wearing white distressed jeans to a party. As mentioned above, white tends to make you look heavier and distressed jeans do not really compliment a middle-aged woman.

Being a Role Model

As a beautiful woman you are also a role model for other women. We live in a world that is far from being perfect. We find ourselves in the midst of a lot of chaos. As members of society, it behooves us all to make whatever contributions we can to our present and future society.

When I began being a professional model, I realized that a lot of what I would be doing was portraying for others what they could be or how they could look. In a fashion show, my job was to show off the designer's clothing. Why? So the designer could sell her creations. Why was she creating these beautiful clothes? So she could help women feel beautiful. So, I was actually being a role "model" showing other women how they could be beautiful.

After several years of modeling, I then became the Talent Director for Cosmo Models Ohio. During that time, part of my job was to teach and coach new models. I showed them how to walk, stand, pose, etc. In short, I showed them how to be beautiful women. To this day, I hear from some of my models who still refer to me as Teacher.

When I became Mrs. China Globe Classic 2015, I learned a great deal from Dr. Tracy Kemble and my other Globe sisters. Being with them helped me develop more self-confidence. They were role models for me.

Recently, as I was walking to a photoshoot in downtown Charlottesville, Virginia (dressed in a very fancy outfit) I heard a young girl say to her mother, "Wow, Mommy! Look at the beautiful lady." It touched my heart. I hoped that I was providing a good example to this child.

We all have an effect on those who surround us. One friend told me "When I got my first job working as the assistant to the CFO, I wore business suits to work. The four girls in the front office used to wear casual clothes, often jeans...but I'd dress up with heels. I had my own office, so I wasn't sitting with them but after a few months, I noticed their clothing changed. By seeing me well-dressed, and looking confident, maybe...they lost the jeans and sweatshirts and began wearing nicer outfits, even dresses on occasions. Within one year, I alone had changed that entire staff and how they dressed. It amazed me. When I started there, it was I who felt out of place, overdressed. But I didn't change. Nothing was ever said to me but I think they got the silent message."

One of my greatest role models is Barbara Tarajczak, the beautiful woman pictured with me at the beginning of this chapter. Barb is not a model or actress. She is a wife, mother, and grandmother. Not long after I came to America, I met Barb and her husband Dick. We quickly became good friends. My husband and I socialized with them and they became my "American parents". Barb has always encouraged and supported me. She and her husband have always been there for us. She invited us to share many family holidays and celebrations. When my husband Edd had a stroke, they drove us to the hospital. Barb is one of the most loving, kind and thoughtful people I have ever met...a truly beautiful woman.

Exercise: What are the three most important things you have learned in this chapter?

1.

2.

3.

Exercise: What are three things you will do as a result of what you have learned?

1.

2.

3.

Exercise: On a scale of 1 to 10, how do you feel about being a beautiful woman now?

1	2	3	4	5	6	7	8	9	10

Less Confident   More Confident

Chapter 7
Relationships

To paraphrase the poet, John Dunne, "No one is an island unto themselves." In other words, human beings are created in community, not in isolation. We juggle the two ideas of dependence and independence. No person is totally independent. When we are born, we are born into a family. It takes a male and a female human being to make another. Whether or not the father and mother are in a working relationship, the child will always be biologically related to both. In a healthy society, the mother and father maintain a supportive relationship with one another and with their offspring.

When we are children, we may have brothers and sisters or we may be a single child. In either event, we must relate to other children. If not siblings, our fellow students when we enter day care or kindergarten. It is through interaction with our family and other people that our personalities are formed. We observe how others relate to one another, and we learn from that. We emulate others.

Positive and Negative Feedback

Throughout our entire lives we are the subject of both positive and negative feedback. As very young children we receive feedback from our family. When we begin our formal education, we receive feedback from teachers and fellow students. Teachers may criticize or praise. Other children may tease, make fun of, reject or accept us. When we become adults, friends, neighbors, fellow workers, extended family members may love, hate, ignore, pay attention to us. All of these will contribute toward the shaping of who we are. Even the society around us will have a profound effect on us.

Our own society through its media and marketing will gie us feedback as to who and what is acceptable and not acceptable. Commercials tell us that we should be slim, trim, young, attractive, brilliant, etc. These same commercials also serve to create criteria for these attributes.

Take a few moments to browse through old television commercials from the 1950s and 60s that can be found on YouTube. Contrast the content of these commercials with some from the 1980s and 90s. What a difference!

Now look through current commercials on television. There is much more diversity. There are many more "average" people portrayed. Yes, there are still ideal people, but they are fewer in number.

Relationships are also important because we need help and support, both to succeed in life and to maintain good mental and physical health. Think about it for a moment. Perhaps you had an aunt or grandmother who had a profound effect on your life. You admired and loved her because of her kindness and love toward you. That relationship helped to form who you are.

Relationships help us to expand both our knowledge and our understanding. Think about the many teachers you had. They passed on to you a vast body of knowledge about how to read and write, how to understand the intricacies of science, the contributions of history, and workings of government and so much more.

While in school, and later in adult life, you have spoken to other people with other points of view and perhaps have changed yours because you saw other aspects of an issue. You might not have agreed with all these other people, but at least your exchange with them helped you to think and to form your own opinions.

When you wanted a job, perhaps you found someone to mentor you, or you had a boss or supervisor who taught you new skills, introduced you to more people, encouraged and supported you. When you found yourself confused, stressed or afraid, perhaps you had a trusted friend or counselor to whom you could turn to both talk out your problems and receive advice and guidance.

At some point in your life, perhaps you met and fell in love with someone and decided that you wanted to share your life with them. You may even have started a family with that person.

All of these have been relationships that have continued to form you. Granted, not all relationships may have been positive or healthy. Some may have been abusive, neglectful, even toxic. But, you have learned something from them.

Exercise: List the three most important positive relationships you have had and explain how they helped you.

1.

2.

3.

Communication

As human beings, we must communicate with other human beings. The ease with which we do this will be one factor in determining our relationships.

In America, even though most of us have a common language (English), we also have subtle dialects, accents, and idiomatic expressions from various parts of the country. There are also rules of grammar that may or may not be used. So, sometimes even Americans don't understand each other.

"After I got through the rotary, I banged a U-ey then went to the packy to pick up some brewskies."

Translation: "When I got to the traffic circle, I made a U-turn then went to the alcoholic beverage store to pick up some beers."

"I ain't got nothing."

Translation: "I do not have anything."

Exercise: List three words or phrases that *you* use that may not be understood by others.

1.

2.

3.

Non-Verbal Communication (Body Language)

Take a few moments to search the Internet for information on body language. It is believed that 80% of all communication between people is done non-verbally. This means, that no matter what language we speak, we often express our thoughts and feelings through body language, otherwise known as non-verbal communication.

We communicate not only with our voices, but also with our bodies. For example, when we make a statement, if we have eye contact with the person to whom we are speaking, that person is more likely to believe us. When we eat a delicious meal, we may smile. This expression helps to convey our enjoyment of the food. If we do not smile, or if we make grimacing faces, these expressions convey disappointment with the food.

Such body language often conveys more accurately how we truly feel than do our words. The study of body language is known as kinesics. Body language is usually controlled by our subconscious mind, although it is possible to consciously use body language once we understand how it works and what various postures and expressions mean.

Imagine that you are sitting across from a person whom you wish to positively influence. Look closely at this person's posture. Does he have his legs crossed? What is she doing with her hands? What kind of expression does he have on his face? Studies have shown that if you assume the same basic posture as this other person, you will be more likely to persuade them.

Exercise: The next time you are in conversation with a friend, watch that person's body language. Below, list three observations about that person's body language.

1.

2.

3.

Exercise: The next time you are in conversation with a friend, be aware of your own body language. Below, list three observations about your body language.

1.

2.

3.

Decisions and Choices

Our lives are profoundly affected by the decisions and choices that we make. This is especially true in our relationships.

When we are children many decisions are made for us. First, it is our parents who make those decisions. Our name, where we live, what clothes we wear are all determined by our parents. While we do not have a choice about what food we will be given, we do have a choice about whether or not we will eat it.

As adults, we are able to make decisions and choices ourselves. However, we do have relationships with others who also make choices and decisions. As we all know, life is not simple.

Exercise: List three decisions that you must make today.

1.

2.

3.

Decisions made by others also have an effect on our lives. Allison applied for a job. She was well qualified and had an excellent resume. She decided that this was the job she wanted, so she worked hard to prepare for the interview. It seemed to go well. However, the next week she was informed that she did not get this job. Someone else had been chosen. The direction of Allison's life now changed because of a decision, a choice. But, it was not her choice. She could not decide *who* would get the job. She could only decide that it was a job *she* wanted.

Imagine that a young woman, who is exceptionally intelligent, completes college and goes to medical school so that she can become a doctor. While in medical school, she falls in love with a man who seems wonderful at first, but turns out to be abusive. She has a child by him, so must drop out of medical school. Her life now takes a very different direction. There were many decisions and choices both for her and for him. Perhaps they were not always healthy choices.

Relationships can nurture or harm, so we must be very careful in making decisions about the people with whom we *choose* to associate. If you want to be a "beautiful" woman, you need to surround yourself with "beautiful" people. In our society, Hollywood has often taught us to think with our hearts and not with our minds. While that may turn out just fine in movies, it is not always that way in real life.

Exercise: What are the three most important things you have learned in this chapter?

1.

2.

3.

Exercise: What are three things you will do as a result of what you have learned?

1.

2.

3.

Exercise: On a scale of 1 to 10, how do you feel about being a beautiful woman now?

1	2	3	4	5	6	7	8	9	10

Less Confident   More Confident

Chapter 8
Making Changes/
Realizing Your Potential

The task now ahead of you is to realize and actualize your potential as a beautiful woman. I would like to give you a three step method to do so. However, before starting to make changes, it is important to assess where you are. Therefore, we will start the change process with an inventory using a tool called the Star of Success.

The Star of Success

Here is a simple, fun technique for setting and achieving goals. There are five major areas of life in which we all want to have some success: Self-image, Health, Wealth, Relationships, and Vocation.

Self-Image

How you feel about yourself profoundly affects every aspect of your life. Do you feel comfortable as a human being? Do you feel good in your skin? What is the difference between how others see you and how you see yourself? These are only a few of the important questions, the answers to which determine who and what we are.

Wealth

Unfortunately, in this life (at least in our society) we need a certain amount of material wealth in order to survive. Both the source of our income and how we choose to spend it will help to determine our lifestyle.

Health

The well-being of our body, mind, and spirit affect everything we do.

Relationships

How we relate to (or don't relate to) other people (family, friends, co-workers, bosses, all of the other people on the planet) is of utmost importance.

Vocation

For our purposes, "vocation" means not only what kind of career or job you have, but also what you do with the rest of your life.

Imagine that each of these five areas is one arm of a five-pointed star, the Star of Success (See the Stars in the back of this workbook). Divide each arm into five segments, each representing the degree of satisfaction with these areas of your life. Focus in on one area at a time, decide whether you are 20%, 40%, 60%, 80%, or 100% satisfied with that area of your life. Using the Star of Success found in the back of this book, and a felt-tipped pen, color in the amount of satisfaction in each arm. Step back and look at the big picture. How balanced is the star? This should give you an idea as to which areas of your life need work.

Now, decide where to start. But...do not start with the area in which you have the smallest percentage of satisfaction. Rather, start with an area in which you have 60% to 80% satisfaction and strive to make it better. Why? You are more likely to have success working on an area in which you already have satisfaction than in an area that is filled with dissatisfaction. Success begets success. So, start small, then after experiencing small success, you can go for bigger success.

When you purchase this book, you also purchase the right to photocopy these stars. I suggest that you go through this exercise on some kind of regular basis, such as weekly, monthly or quarterly, so that you can monitor your progress. Obviously, percentages will vary each time, depending on what is happening in your life. The goal is balance.

Exercise: Using the Star of Success, measure your level of satisfaction in the five areas of your life and list them below.

Self-image	Percentage of satisfaction:
Relationships	Percentage of satisfaction:
Vocation	Percentage of satisfaction:
Health	Percentage of satisfaction:
Wealth	Percentage of satisfaction:

Step 1 – Education

Both Albert Einstein and Socrates have been credited with saying, "The more I know, the more I realize how much I don't know." Before, during, and after deciding what changes you want to make, it is always best to learn as much as you can about how to be a better person.

Before deciding what changes you want to make, find out about the benefits as well as the pitfalls (and possible side effects) of whatever this change may be. This is true especially for changes that may require surgery.

Education can take many forms. You can begin by consulting people who are experienced in whatever field may be appropriate. Talk to models, doctors, beauticians, fitness instructors, etc., so that you can obtain qualified guidance.

Read books that may be appropriate. You have started with this one! Check the list of recommended reading in the back of this workbook. If you have difficulty reading, try audiobooks.

Go online and seek out information. YouTube is an excellent source. You are able to see actual video tutorials on almost any subject from how to apply makeup to how to walk and talk.

Take classes or private instruction. Classes and workshops not only give you information, but they also allow you the opportunity to interact with like-minded people. Some of these people may later become friends and a part of your support system.

Exercise: Find at least three educational opportunities to help you become a more beautiful woman. List them below.

1.

2.

3.

Step 2 - Setting Goals

A wise man once said, "You will never hit the bullseye if you do not have a target." In order to effectively make changes in your life, it is important to set goals. And those goals should be SMART: **S**pecific, **M**easurable, **A**ttainable, **R**ealistic, and **T**imely.

Let us assume that you have decided that you want to lose weight. To make this a SMART goal, you will need to fine tune it. Vague goals that you hope to reach some time are not truly goals. They are dreams. The more concrete you make your goal (the bull's eye) the more likely you are to reach it. Why do you think that most targets have different colored rings? If the target were simply a large white circle, it would be more difficult to aim.

Exercise: Create a SMART weight loss goal (even if you do not really need i.).

Specific / Exactly how much do you want to lose? 10 pounds? 15? 20?	
Measurable / How can you measure the amount you are losing on a daily/ weekly/monthly basis? How often will you measure?	
Attainable / Is this something you can really do? What steps do you need to take? Are there obstacles such as health? time? cost?	
Realistic / Is losing a lot of weight very quickly something you can *really* do? Maybe you need to "make haste slowly." Will you be motivated? Can you stick to your plan?	
Timely / When will you accomplish this? In one week? One month? Six months? There is no urgency if you leave this wide open. Pick a date.	

Now that you have tried this exercise, choose another goal – one that *you* would like to reach.

Exercise: Based on the lowest percentage arm of your Star of Success, create a SMART goal for yourself.

Goal:

Specific	
Measurable	
Attainable	
Realistic	
Timely	

Once you have set a SMART goal, you need to ask yourself what will keep you motivated to reach the goal. The stronger the motivation, the more likely you are to accomplish the goal. I would like to suggest two important tools to creating and maintaining motivation: reward and accountability.

Think about when you were a child. Imagine two simple scenarios.

Scenario 1: Mother tells you that when you eat all your vegetables then you will have dessert.

Scenario 2: Mother tells you that if you do not eat all your vegetables then you will not have dessert.

Which scenario would create motivation for you? Probably the first, because it is phrased with positive expectation ("when" rather than "if"). It also gives you something positive to look forward to. Dessert! Scenario 2 implies that you might not eat your vegetables (because of that word "if"). It is also based on punishment. No dessert! Are you more motivated by reward or punishment?

Exercise: Thinking about the SMART goal you created above, what kind of reward could you give yourself for achieving it?

Be sure that this reward is also SMART and responsible. If you are trying to stick to a healthy diet, do not say that you will reward yourself with a big slice of cake for losing ten pounds. Buy yourself a new outfit. Treat yourself to a movie or a concert. Try to make the reward a celebration of your success. Go out and show off what you have accomplished!

Accountability

Accountability is another important tool to create and maintain motivation. You are more likely to accomplish a goal if you have told someone else that you intend to reach that goal. Your source of accountability could be a sibling, parent, friend, or even a coach. When you have accomplished your goal, you can also celebrate that goal with this person.

The advantage of having a coach is that such a person can also assist you in creating SMART goals, and will continue to guide and support you as you strive toward making positive changes in your life. There are life coaches, fitness coaches, career coaches, health coaches, relationship coaches, financial coaches (aka financial advisers) etc.

If you do not have a coach, you may want to consider finding multiple sources of accountability for yourself. If weight loss is a goal, you may want to join a weight control group that has periodic meetings. Or, you might even want to post your goals on social media, thus making all your "friends" a source of accountability.

Exercise: Find a source (or sources) of accountability for yourself.

Exercise: Do an online search for various coaches in your area. List URLs below.

Obstacles

Regardless of how motivated you may be, sometimes there are things that get in the way of accomplishing your goals. For example, your goal may be to go to a gym three days a week. However, you have just contracted the flu and are in bed for an entire week. Or, perhaps a good friend has invited you on an all-expense-paid week's vacation.

Some obstacles may be preventable, others not. Some can be worked around, others not.

Step 3 – Imagination

In 1960, Dr. Maxwell Maltz, a plastic surgeon, discovered that many of his patients wanted to alter their appearance in order to become more successful. Perhaps a smaller nose or less sagging here and there would make them a better salesperson, actor, lawyer, etc. After a while, Dr. Maltz concluded that many of these people did not really need plastic surgery, they actually needed an adjustment to their self-image. He then developed a system for improving self-image and wrote a book entitled **Psycho-Cybernetics** that outlined a system for making such changes.

Dr. Maltz used the basic tools of imagination and visualization, which we will also be using. These are based on principles that have been used for centuries in many forms, including prayer, meditation, psychotherapy, and hypnotherapy. These techniques are often successful in facilitating change because they start with change on the "inside" which then results in a change on the "outside."

The 19th-century psychologist Emile Coue recommended saying to yourself "Day by day, I am getting better and better." You can paraphrase this by mentally repeating "Day by day, I am getting more and more beautiful" several times every day.

Because the subconscious mind is such a powerful tool in creating the person you are, let's use imagination as a tool for making changes. Your self-image is of utmost importance. It is your imagination that forms your self-image.

Exercise: Use the following imaginative exercise on a daily basis. Repeat at least 2 or 3 times a day for the next two weeks.

Imagination is best used when you are relaxed. Find a comfortable chair, close your eyes, take a deep breath and as you exhale, mentally say the word "calm." Take another deep breath and as you exhale, mentally say the word "peace." Take a third deep breath and as you exhale, mentally say the word "relax."

Now begin to use your imagination. Mentally see yourself standing in front of a mirror. Imagine that you see yourself as a beautiful, confident, powerful woman. Imagine that you are wearing the kind of clothes that make you feel beautiful. See yourself as the ideal you.

Mentally say, "I am a beautiful woman" at least three times.

Imagine that you turn and walk away from the mirror. You see yourself on a stairway leading up. There are 10 steps. At the top of the stairs is a platform, a landing. See yourself walking up the steps. Each time you take a step, you mentally say, "I am a beautiful woman."

When you reach the top and stand on the platform, you see your family and friends. You see people you have known in the past. You see people who are now and who have been important to you. You look out at them and they are looking back at you with smiles. You say to them, "I am a beautiful woman." All of these people applaud. Imagine how that would feel. All of these people are affirming you as a beautiful woman.

By repeating this exercise on a regular basis, you are feeding your subconscious mind with images and feelings that are positively reinforcing your new self-image. Years of negative thoughts and feelings are now being replaced.

"I think I am a beautiful woman; therefore, I am a beautiful woman."

Let this be your "mantra".

Bonus Step – Visualization

In addition to mental, imaginative reinforcement of your goals, there is another tool that may be helpful. It helps if you can see your success. There are many names for this technique. I prefer "The ME Poster". Get yourself a piece of cardstock or poster board, a large felt-tip pen and lots of women's magazines. At the top of your poster, write the words "I AM A BEAUTIFUL WOMAN" in big letters. Find pictures in the magazines (or go online and find pictures, print them, and cut them out) that show the kind of success that you want. Pictures of models; successful, powerful women, Olympic athletes, actresses, etc. Put photos of yourself taken when you looked and felt beautiful. Near the pictures, write the attributes of a beautiful woman.

Put your Me Poster in a prominent location such as your refrigerator door, bedroom mirror, etc. This will give you physical, conscious reinforcement on a daily basis.

Exercise: What are the three most important things you have learned in this chapter?

1.

3.

Exercise: What are three things that you will do as a result of what you have learned?

.

2.

3.

Exercise: On a scale of 1 to 10, how do you feel about being a beautiful woman now?

| 1 | 2 | 3 | 4 | 5 | 6 | 7 | 8 | 9 | 10 |

Less Confident   More Confident

Li Wang

CHAPTER 9

The Journey Continues

The journey to becoming the beautiful woman you already are is not something that ends when you have completed this workbook. This journey is one that continues throughout the rest of your life. As persons, we are constantly changing, as does the world in which we live. Because of this, the very meaning of being a beautiful woman can change as well. We all have individual successes and failures, set- backs and moves forward, peaks and valleys in our lives. It is how we respond to and adapt to these events that forms our inner and outer beauty.

I would like to share a story with you that I hope you will find inspiring. Several years ago, when I was beginning my career as a model/actor, I saw a casting call for the role of a wife/mother in a music video to be shot in Pittsburgh, PA. At that time, we were living near Cleveland, OH. This would be a non-speaking role, so I would not need to worry about my English. There was a brief synopsis of the story for the video. A young business man would be telling about his life in a rush and confusing world. He would be seen with his wife and children, going off to work, then coming home only to discover that his world was really just a fantasy.

I thought that I would like to try, but I was not very confident at that time. The casting call was looking for an Asian woman and did not specify an age. There would be an audition in Pittsburgh, then shooting would be a few days after. We were required to send a headshot (head and shoulders photo) and a resume.

My husband Edd and I had a lot of discussion about this before I applied. We would have to drive about three hours each way and there would be no guarantee that I would get the role. If I did, we would need to drive back to Pittsburgh two days later. I was very unsure. Besides, I felt that maybe I was too old for this role. At the audition, photos would be taken that would be used for a full-size cut-out, so I would need to wear an appropriate wardrobe, and wear the same when I returned for the shoot.

It was Edd who insisted that I try. So, I chose a pretty white and blue dress, and off we went to meet with the director. We were told that the music video would feature a popular rapper named Mac Miller (real name Malcolm McCormack) and the title of the video would be *Brand Name*. I was not into rap music, so was not familiar with him.

We showed up at the audition, and the director and producer were already excited. They had seen my resume and photo and felt that I was perfect for the role. I was thrilled! They took photos of me and we drove home very excited.

When we returned, we met Malcolm. He was a gentleman. I discovered that he was about twenty years younger than I. What a surprise! He was the same age as my adult son, and yet I would be playing the role of his wife. What a boost to my self-confidence!

Hopefully, this workbook has now given you some direction, some motivation. The exercises in this book are not meant to be "once and done" but a framework that you may use over and over. This is why I suggested early on that you do the exercises with a pencil. I recommend that you go back every six months or so, look at what you wrote before, and make any appropriate changes.

Here is only a partial list of the things that you can do to continue your growth as a beautiful woman.

- Use this workbook again and again.

- Use the imagination and visualization exercises on a regular basis.

- Use the Star of Success to monitor your growth.

    – Do things that you enjoy. Remember that success begets success. Accomplish something new and different. This will boost your self-confidence.

    – Build relationships with other beautiful women. You may need their support...and *they may need yours*.

    - Do some volunteer work so that you can share your life and empower others.

    – Educate yourself. Read books about self-confidence, beauty, fashion, and etiquette.

    – Listen to audio books that are inspirational and motivational.

You are *always becoming* the beautiful woman that you already are.

Final Exercise: What are the three most important things you have learned in this workbook?

1.

2.

3.

Final Exercise: What are three things that you will do as a result of what you have learned?

1.

2.

3.

Exercise: On a scale of 1 to 10, how do you feel about being a beautiful woman now?

1	2	3	4	5	6	7	8	9	10

Less Confident   More Confident

Suggested Reading

Empowerment is S.E.X.Y: Learning Healthy Selfish and the 4 Secrets to Making Life and Love Work, Dr. Tracy Kemble, 2014

How Not to Care What People Think: The 4 Secrets to Staying True to Self, Dr. Tracy Kemble, 2017

How to Win Friends and Influence People, Dale Carnegie, 1936

Nigel Barker's Beauty Equation: Revealing a Better and More Beautiful You, Nigel Barker, 2010

The Power of Body Language, Joe Navarro, 2009

The Power of Positive Thinking, Norman Vincent Peale, 1952

Psycho-Cybernetics, Maxwell Maltz, 1960

Acknowledgments

There are many people who have directly or indirectly contributed to this workbook, and whom I would like to thank for their support, guidance, and advice.

First and foremost, Edd Schultz, my husband and editor. Edd has been with me and behind me since 2006, when we were married in China. He is a writer, actor, model, photographer, coach, and teacher. The author of several books, it was his writing and editing skills that allowed me to put my thoughts into words. He has also been (and continues to be) my major source of moral support and encouragement.

Dr. Tracy Kemble, my inspiration. Ever since I became a part of the Mrs. Globe family, my self-confidence has sky rocketed. It was Dr. Tracy's belief in me that provided the impetus for me to write this workbook. I will be forever grateful to her.

Wang Mei, Writer, Director, Producer for her encouragement and support.

Rita Doyle Walsh, Dr. Vanni Murthi, Nancy Westberg, Skylar Lippiat, Barbara Tarajaczk, and Mary Trela, my readers. Another pair of eyes is always necessary when writing a book. These beautiful women also added valuable insights.

Skylar Lippiat, my teacher. Before I began my career as a professional model and actor, Skylar was my teacher at Barbizon of Akron. Despite my language difficulties, she gave me the training and boosted my self-confidence to new heights.

Photo Credits: Delores Couceiro (p. iv), Adrienne Eichner (pp. 47, 53, 55), Jessica Lowman (p. vi), Jim Metrisin (56), Eric Mull (Cover, p. 96), Gregory Pendolino (p. 87), Edd Schultz (pp. 10, 11, 17, 35, 75)

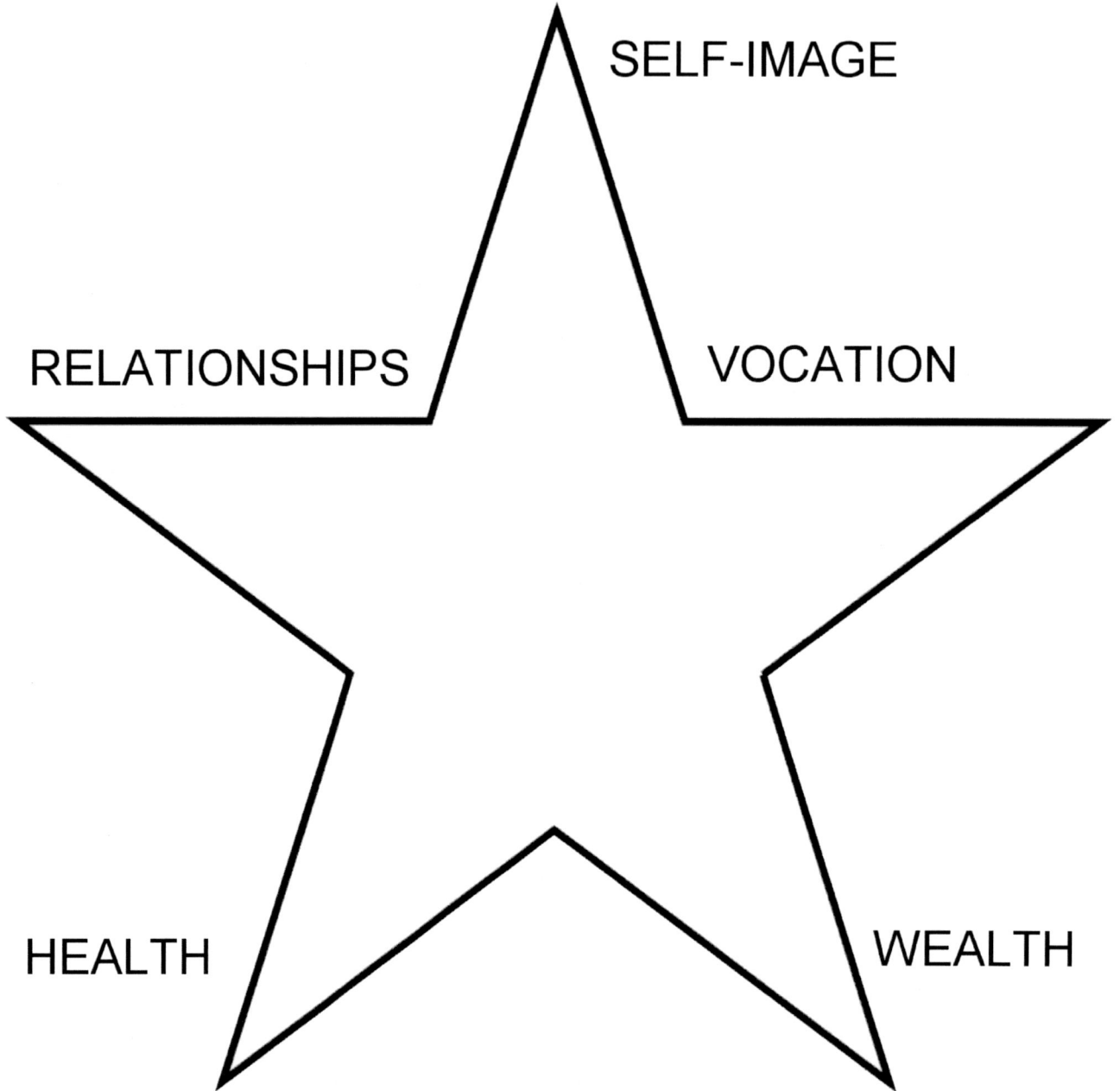

SELF-IMAGE

RELATIONSHIPS

VOCATION

HEALTH

WEALTH

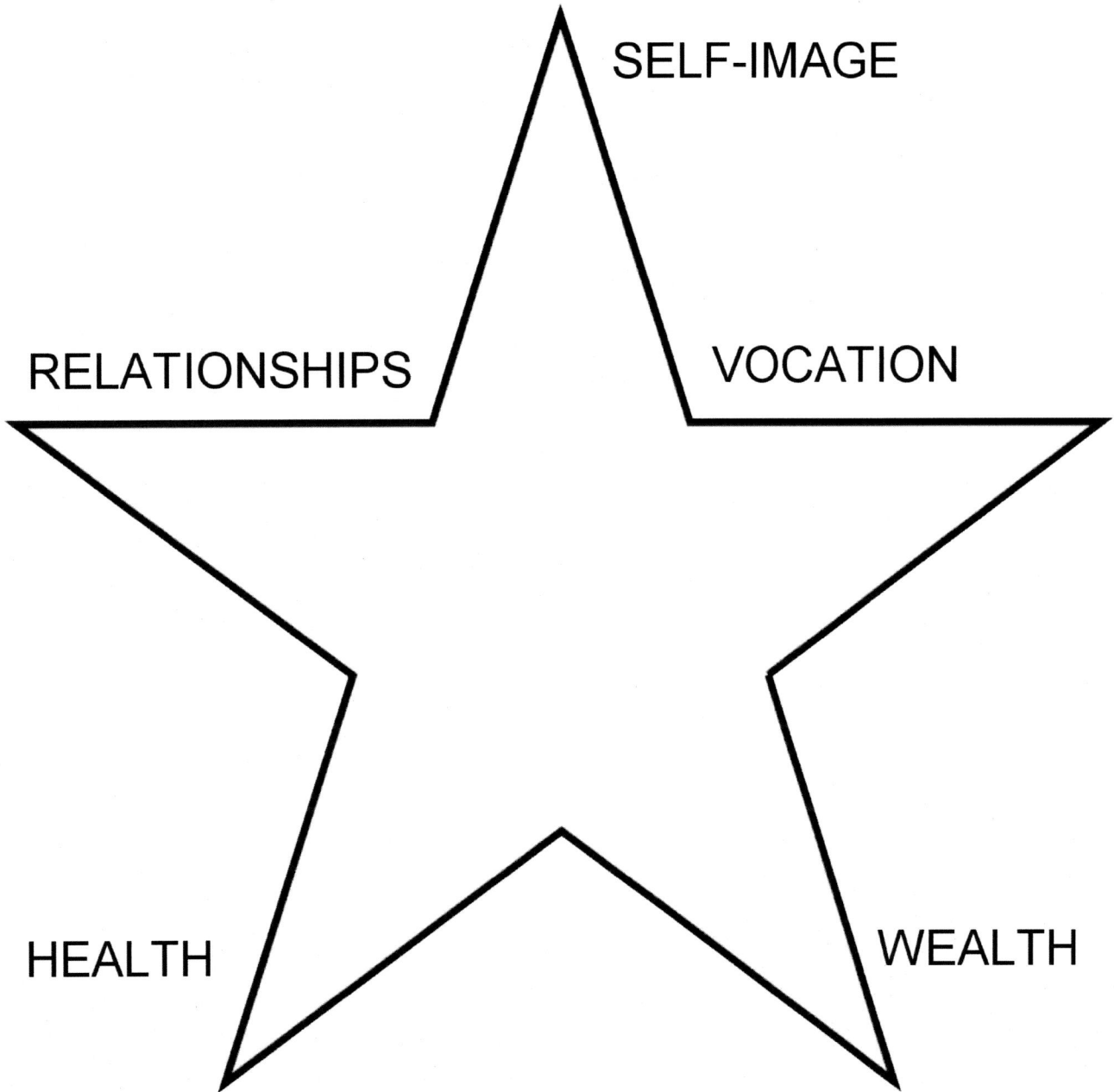

SELF-IMAGE

RELATIONSHIPS

VOCATION

HEALTH

WEALTH

About the Author

For more than twenty years, Li Wang was a successful music and dance teacher in China, living a humble life. In 2006, she married an American man, and waited 18 months to receive a visa to come to the U.S. She arrived not speaking very much English. Within a few years, she learned English, worked numerous jobs, studied modeling and acting, and finally became a successful model, modeling coach and actress, Mrs. China Globe Classic 2015, Talent Director for Cosmo Models Ohio, a judge for various fashion shows and beauty pageants, as well as being an entrepreneur by starting her own company, EDMay – The Healthy Living Way. Li has devoted herself to empowering women of all ages and ethnicities. "I have always liked beauty in my life. It makes me very happy. I would like to share this with others." She currently resides in Virginia with her husband Edd Schultz, and their Yorkie.

Made in the USA
Middletown, DE
15 January 2019